October on Nantucket

A POETRY COLLECTION
TO REMEMBER THE "FAR AWAY LAND"

*For Michael & Wendy Hayne,
& their boys —
Ben & Peter —
with love,
Tracy Leddy*

October on Nantucket

A POETRY COLLECTION
TO REMEMBER THE "FAR AWAY LAND"

BY TRACY LEDDY

October on Nantucket

A POETRY COLLECTION
TO REMEMBER THE "FAR AWAY LAND"

by Tracy Leddy

2nd Edition
Copyright © 2012, Quail Hill Publishing

Illustrations by: Michael Raysson
Cover photo by: Greg Hinson
Design & development by: Mind's Eye Communications, LLC

1st Edition
Copyright © 1987, Quail Hill Communications

Originally printed and typeset by:
The Sant Bani Press, Tilton, NH

All rights reserved. No part of this book may be reproduced in any form by any electronic or mechanical means including photocopying, recording, or information storage and retrieval without permission in writing from the author.

ISBN-13: 978-1481014540
ISBN-10: 1481014544

www.quailhillpublishing.com
Email: info@quailhillpublishing.com

Give feedback on the book at:
feedback@quailhillpublishing.com

Printed in U.S.A

For AJ

TABLE OF CONTENTS

I. SUMMER

13 The Nantucket Dump

14 Tuckernuck

15 The Crabbing Bridge

17 The Outing

18 At Smith's Point

19 Monomoy

20 The Old Mill

21 Tower Beach

22 At Quidnet: Tern Nesting Area

23 Madaket

24 Nantucket Whale Watch

25 Beach Scene: Boy With Blue Kite

26 Steps Beach

27 Driving Back From The Finast

28 Hinckley Lane

29 Sunset At Smith's Point

30 Hands To Work

31 Dark Thoughts

32 In One Corner Of The Garden

33 The Conversation

34 At My Friend's House

35 In The Cabin

36 Silent Supper

37 Between The Thunderstorms

38 In The Current

39 Eel Point

40 Down From Boundless Joy

41 More About Monomoy

42 Coskata

43 Swimming

44 Surfcasters At Smith's Point

45 Just Below the Gazebo

46 New Lane: The Flaggy Meadow

47 Evening At The White Elephant

48 Over Dinner

49 Summer Song

II. FALL

53 Labor Day

54 Madaket Clambake

55 The Assault

56 The Fall

57 After Nantucket There Is Only God

58 Cisco Beach: Hurricane

59 Not Yet

60 Attachment

61 Portrait Of A Young Man

62 Polpis Harbor

63 October On Nantucket

64 Water Color

65 Thanksgiving 1984

66 At Tom Never's Head

67 Approaching The Cave

III. WINTER

71 Nantucket Monochrome

72 Interior Landscape

73 Like A Beacon On High

74 'Sconset Beach

75 Surfside: State Forest

76 The Flotation Device

78 New Year's Eve: 1986

79 On Lincoln's Birthday

80 In Our Back Yard

81 At Hummock Pond

82 Long Pond

83 Beyond The Shells

IV. SPRING

87 What Happened To Great Point Light

88 The Jetties

89 Bright Green

90 More In Madaket

91 March Storm

92 Easter: Wind With Junipers

93 Daffodils

94 More Lessons

95 The Daffodil Festival

97 April On Nantucket

98 Much More Than Spring

99 Easy Street Basin

100 The Bottle Plant

101 At Cisco Beach: "The Ark" Is Claimed By The Sea

102 A Gardener's Catalogue

103 Still Life With Daffodils

THE STARS ARE PERCOLATING THROUGH THE DARK WE ARE THOSE STARS AND SOME NIGHT LIGHT ALL WILL BE LIGHT

I. SUMMER

The Nantucket Dump

Countless gulls pattern the blue   or fight
viciously over the latest pickings
a charterboat's bountiful stink of fish
Cars   vans   jeeps and trucks are in and out all day
The ancient tractor coughs and strains
at its labors   moving steadily rising mountains
around and around and around   Loose papers
bloom on the surrounding moors
poor cousins to honeysuckle and heather
bayberry   blueberry   lily   broom and multiflora rose
The old caretaker surveys this rotting domain
smokes his everpresent pipe and dreams
of Maddaquecham Valley after five
gentle   silent   peaceful and green

Behind my eyes
this place is closing down for good
Dumping   of any kind   is no longer allowed
The birds have all but deserted   Tractor's
been abandoned   Terrain is fixed at last
Atop the highest mound the caretaker now stands
already busy with a shovel   He's been told
by one he trusts there are diamonds far beneath
so he ignores both stench and slime
and goes digging   digging   Lost his pipe long ago
Spends more and more time here   growing stronger
and stronger   Doesn't care how long he takes
how tired he gets
He wants to find those diamonds

How much he wants those diamonds

Tuckernuck

The stars are percolating through the dark
We are those stars and
some night all will be light

The fallen stars are in the sea
wash up on sand
to trail the departing fisherman
a second Sirius briefly seen
                    Altair   Deneb   Vega
or are they sparks from holy feet
his light tread shedding brightness
Bathing toes spray up a lesser
Milky Way and countless constellations

Back into the ocean they go
and back up into the sky to where
                    slowly
the stars are percolating through the dark
We are those stars and
some night
           all will be light

The Crabbing Bridge

A small neonlimegreen plastic pail's
                              been left
empty
at the water's edge;
A clamorous focus in this placid place.
I sit and stare and wonder
was there perhaps some lovefilled child
                                   of five
(still at one with all of life)
made so upset
by a caught crab's outcry
he had to be taken abruptly away.

Tall dull grasses slither in the rising
                              east wind.
Cattails clatter among multiflora roses.
Thick quilted clouds hang low and grey;
we should soon have rain.

The Outing

It was to be a little expedition
he in his rowboat   I in mine
just offshore
to catch a few blues
out past the surfmen's furthest cast
back in time for dinner

But soon
I am mid-ocean   alone   without oars
the sea fast covering the sky

At Smith's Point

A few feet above this fine white sand
a butterfly dances madly past us
                          away
from moorlands   houses and gardens
away from eelgrass and beachpeas
down to the naked end of the strand
over the channel and out to sea

the hand in the violent wind behind us
pushing
pushing

Monomoy

From our (second storey) bedroom window I look out
on mostly green: dense shrubs close below the house, then
a stand of tall purple wands — too feathery to be cattails—
then an expanse of salt marsh at high tide. The water is
calm; gilded near the sandstreaked banks by the waning sun.
A grizzled fisherman among his lobster traps puttputts down
the meander. The Old Mill dominates the low horizon; its
sails are still. There is a slight haze. Gulls, a single
white heron, whole families of ducks, and other birds dip
and call.

The tranquility is breathtaking.

The Old Mill

Four great sails fill and turn
Below   one stone is beauty
the other wheel's suffering
                                    I
a cast of corn between

Tower Beach

The old harbor is enclosed now
Cattails beachgrass and tons
of fine white sand bar the ocean's way

We climb high hot desert dunes
Like Balboa facing the Pacific
hearts catch every time at first sight
of stenciled sails low against the blue
and vast calm

The man floats wide open
to the light
              til the wind shifts
and a fog drifts in from Eel Point

Beyond dense mats of bearberries
fires of poison ivy
the pink mallows dance

At Quidnet: Tern Nesting Area

High southwest wind this bright day
blowing steadily fifteen to twenty knots   gusting
up to forty
Where to get away from it   Northeast
on the beach below the dunes at Quidnet

The sea was flat and vast and welcoming
as a mother
                but it was on top of a low bluff
facing 'Sacacha Pond the paternal embrace came
In that strong warm buffeting   intimate as sex
or breathing   gone was the years-old trauma
of treelimbs crashing seconds behind kin and friends
of needlepricks in horizontal rain

                                Oh may I stand
before the stormobstructed inner door
                                        long and still
as I did one rapturous afternoon in island sand

Madaket

Lately
much greyness and rain   But today
the sea is lapis   azure   aquamarine
near waves pale sunspattered jade

Up the beach two young boys leap
fling arms high and wide
lie prostrate in the sinking foam
even as we
before entering the light

Nantucket Whale Watch

Something of a pilgrimage   this
Forty self-selected rare birds on board
to seek and find the elusive Simurgh
he of flippers and giant flukes
The naturalist   full of facts tales and
observations   our hoopoe

Like patient meditators   our busy eyes
rinsed by fog   shooting stars and endless
water   we watch and wait
        watch and wait

Shoals   shearwaters   petrels   hammerheads
dolphins   tuna   all draw delighted cries and comments
but in the presence of these great half-
hidden shapes we have come so far to see
a holy hush descends
Our hearts reel out like harpoon lines
for they are sacred music   each graceful
slow rotation   each plumed exhalation
part of a rare enchanting tune
Like one single listener we strain
to catch the briefest note
In every reverent glance some small expiation
for our bloody greedy past

Beach Scene: Boy With Blue Kite

It is my husband's mood I watch   spirals
spins   dips   lifts   loops and sudden
crashes   A wonder the frail thing does not
shatter
His heart is sore from wanting   wanting
Surgery cannot heal the knife he faces
The scent of roses does not reach him
nor sails in the bay   Honeysuckle cannot
knock him off the crushed shell path
the pale fine sand   spirals   spins
dips   lifts   loops and sudden crashes
a wonder the frail thing does not shatter

Steps Beach

Grey sea   grey sky   a curving strand
The instant kingdom of the rain
from groins to jetties   empty   mine

Is this old steep wooden staircase
hemmed in by roses   honeysuckle
columbine less than Paradise
Today the drunken buzzing sentries
too have fled   I pass unchallenged
onto pocked damp sand and quickly into
where I am island   seal   whale   wave
exultant

A slash of light below dark clouds
like the space beneath the door
in a colonial house
Boats steam toward it

I wait for it to open   open

Driving Back From The Finast

What do you miss most   living on
Nantucket   asked our oldest friend
over candlelit dinner on the porch
facing gardens   moors   shingled houses
sunsets   Mountains   said mine host

And late this Sunday afternoon the sky
is filled with dark escarpments
behind bits of flying mist   It is Ireland's
Wicklow Hills   Glen Coe   Loch Linhe   It is
Virginia's Blue Ridge   Rajpur looking toward
                                        Mussoorie
You can see the thin waterfalls
the wealth of trees
                        or is it another glimpse
of the inner planes   the veil lifting
lifting   and the heart

Those heights I will climb
On those summits stand   and sing

Hinckley Lane

His daily prescribed walks
seem to be taking us
into new territory   a rough
tender playfulness   an openness
unknown in twenty-five years
Is it because he thinks he is
going to die   soon   the light
heartedness finally comes

This densely hemmed in sandy lane
becomes at dusk a silent cloister
Privet archways hide side paths
children's voices   banging screen doors
Through more tall scented privet
narrower   narrower at the end
like the needle's eye   then suddenly
out
among the daises   roses
facing only sea and sky

A single feather of a boat
rests below near shore
Dark scrolls unroll toward us
from the north
One white gull glides   high

Sunset At Smith's Point

If I could invite the entire world
down behind the houses
to watch this placid shimmering sea
turn turquoise   peach and lavender
while vivid grasses barely wave
and gulls stand or sit like decoys
the only dark
as the light flows toward me

there would be no war

Hands To Work

for Siobhain Klawetter

This is where I would like to be always
inside a silent, busy garden
amid butterflies, blossoms, waterdrop worlds
in small green cups,
my hands smelling of compost and rosemary
my eyes trained on any secret red
swellings, the least weed.
A quilted sky full of rain above me;
just enough breeze to keep mosquitoes away,
and the inner music louder than bird-
song or nearby surf.

I am richer than Croesus:
tomatoes, berries my rubies, sapphires;
old dung my gold.

Dark Thoughts

You black and reeking butterflies
single or entire families, stay out
of my garden (which is really His;
I only tend it, await Him).
Your briefest presence threatens blight;
wherever you alight and, God forbid, suck,
I suffer instantaneous destruction.

With the net of my attention
I shall capture every one of you, impale you
to study your characteristics, history.
Even the soil in here is sweet;
after much hard work everything's flourishing;
do not intrude, I say,
or meet certain doom.

In One Corner of the Garden

A pumpkin vine's caught hold
of a climbing Peace rose.
Let go, let go, I protest,
carefully extricating it
from each tiny tenacious tendril,
Then begin to cry:
I am that struggling bloom,
and all which surrounds me
                the vine.

The Conversation

You enter   anxious   uneasy
sink quickly into your favorite chair
opposite mine
                   and wait for words
But in the draft of air
behind you
we two
are suddenly three
The Holy One has come among us
eyes like the void before creation
every pore exuding peace
                        I turn
toward that throbbing space
like a parched plant in a deluge
like a sunflower on a blazing August day
In this heavy singing stillness
what is there to think
who is there to be
what is there to say

From: Visiting the Vineyard

At My Friend's House
For Pat Newick

Small ship beached in deep woods,
Steep gravel steps,
Heavy door, golden porthole,

Stop.

Five years ago a saint stood here,
spoke of God to my friend's tall mate,
as the long living room filled with grace
and the dining room bridge trembled
with his blessing.

It is unchanged.

We sit up late over cups of tea
at first like shy village girls beside
a stream; brides to be,
bleaching, bleaching our own
wedding sheets, winding sheets,
but as the holy spaces in our conversation
widen,
we become tiny island planes
leaping eagerly
into clouds of Sound.

From: Visiting the Vineyard

In The Cabin

It's a privilege to sleep here
I told my friend
Alone in deep woods   no wind
no sound   just prayer
                              But
in the middle of the stars
one came and lay on top of me
like a beached whale
I bore that weight like patient sand
until hot furtive urgent hands
began

Then I screamed and jabbed and bit
and pulled his curly dark hair
Hurled him off my narrow cot

What are you doing
I wanted to see you and you
were asleep
You could have spoken   touched my toes
or my shoulder
He hung his head and left
through the only swollen locked
accidentally from the outside door

Oh mattress   I am asking you
What really happened

Silent Supper

Sunflowers bow
Robins perch on the short white pickets
which define my garden or hop
across the freshcut lawn
A pheasant family attacks our blueberry
patch   scratching and leaping
A late August sun slides slowly down a singing sky
Eternity unfolds

A resident rabbit sits unblinking while I eat
then I remain unmoving as he grazes
Both vegetarians   his the simpler diet
Relies wholly on Providence
I can learn from him but does he too now feel
this ringing stillness press around him
rush through every sinew and cell
like a millrace   making him shake   shake
with joy
as the last membrane breaks

We live in a beam of light and strength
which is annihilating
Lovingly cradled for an operation guaranteed
to dissolve the I entirely
in Sound

Sunflowers bow
Robins perch or hop
A pheasant family scratches   leaps
while a late August sun slides slowly down a singing
sky and
eternity unfolds

Between Thunderstorms

Oh-oh: one part sphinx to two parts
Jabba the Hut, fat odd-eyed Silas Tyger,
Neighborhood predator,
Is lying down at his ease
In the center of my back yard
Lawn.
                       He's
Acting as though he owns
The place; hasn't a care in this world,
But a pulse in that long fluffy tail's
A telling metronome:
Something's definitely up.

(Usually he is furtive, stealthy, and sly:
I've grown resigned to noting
His passage across the edge of the grass,
Or him skulking under the side deck,
intent on yet
Another hunting expedition
Regardless of the season.

Sometimes he's successful:
I've found the remaining feathers.)

A few feet closer to me
In one green declivity, I finally
Can discern
The pair of small flattened ears
That has caught the cat's
Attention:
A tiny stonestill rabbit,
Hoping against hope
More soaking rain will fall
                       Before

In The Current

Out on the north side of Esther's the weed
was thick   the water low   my first swim merely
dutiful

At a friend's suggestion I tried
riding the swift current around the island's head
like a pale sea flower   a bit of eelgrass
to the restraining bar   Never the fear of being
swept into a sharkinfested channel   on out
to open sea
Up the beach   then in again   rejoicing   blue
lipped and shivering
remembering another current I enter
without moving
Never the thought of hand hold   toe hold
the desire to wallow in the shallows or clamber up
the sand
wanting only to rest in its flow forever
wherever it takes me

Years ago when you left this world
and disappeared into that other ocean   people wept
and cried   Alas he has abandoned us
                                        But
from my place on shore I saw you reemerge far out
and sit down on a tiny island with your eyes closed
I pushed through the grieving ones   dove in
and swam and swam until I stood beside you

Hello   oh hello   I have come

Eel Point

I keep thinking
I've lived here long enough
seen all there is to see in two times
four radiant seasons on this holy isle
but then there's fog coming in at Eel Point
                                 low tide
In quiet water   and behind flimsy clouds
the sun's a double blast furnace
Turreted Tuckernuck's fast disappearing in rising
                                 whiteness
(Threemile distant Smith's Point's already invisible)
Gulls ride lines of shimmering diamond light while
out on one of the many bars a family of shadow
puppets   six   all sizes   cavorts and looks for shells
Nearer shore hermit crabs scruffle around my bare
toes   No two oratories alike
I could wade to Muskeget   the Vineyard   heaven
at least to the old wreck

A jet hums high
The late afternoon ferry throbs across the horizon
Straight courses through chaos

Everything before me is a finger pointing
                              Oh
I need no other text

Down From Boundless Joy

This sand eel's about three   clad
only in ropes of seaweed
as he knees up the beach at the edge
of the waves
              Crowing and gasping
he wriggles and rolls   clutches damp land
lest he fall off

Me for that mythic bird
who hatches breeds and dies in the sky

Neither highdiving nor dreams will suffice
another day   One merely seems to fly

Ah, God   Over me the great white bull
no longer holds sway   Slowly
but surely I am leaving his passionate domain

"Like a hair out of butter"

More About Monomoy

Low and west Muskegat basks
in slatesilverblue like a giant sunfish
Opens one eye and smiles
                          A few breaths further
our slightlymorethan birdbody
drops
down
       Oh, only God could write the poem
that is this island

                          I feast on
saltmarsh at floodtide   rose-encrusted cottages
hydrangeas big as Osage oranges and
mostly every blue   a field of longdead daisies
now a festival of king's candle
pheasant squawking in the blossoming privet
rabbits browsing and grooming in a pasture
ears glowing red in the notyetsetting sun

The lapping waves are warm
the masts in the harbor are many   Oh, hear
the prayer wheels of Nantucket below a horizon
pierced with spires
                          Always the delirium of light
on water   that diamond path through a shining hole
in the sky
            Oh, only God could write the poem
that is this island

Coskata

for John Brock and Marsha Fader

Mostly sky and high winds   Some few
brave gulls and even braver roses
Acres of acquiescent eelgrass
ragged gorse   bayberry and cedar
A curve of sand   A white light at the Point

One giant leap away from the pebbled beach
a little manywindowed cabin   up high
spare and snug and strong enough
for any storm
                    Light pours through it
until the gold stone drops back into the sea

Oh, let there be here a stripping cleansing
wind to prepare me
for the unending sun

Swimming

I am increasingly reluctant to leave
the water   Each day
I try to dive float stroke further down this
rose-adorned beach

I am tired of the dry land of my mind

Tonight when we meet together and begin to sing
I am swimming swimming in another sea
feeling the surge of its waves in words   notes
my own breath
Then buoyant in listening silence
never a thought of touching bottom
of wading ashore
                              More stroking
light as spindrift
while I walk the crowsfly mile home

Surfcasters at Smith's Point

They are waiting to become monks
these silent or rowdy ones
at the surf's edge   especially
in a south wind
Minds free of the world
Eyes focused only on the end of a rod
Patient   persevering   gentle
enduring   A splendid sunset's never
lost on them

Surely they are most pleasing to God
as they throw their catch back
give it away
Surely they are waiting to become monks

Just Below The Gazebo

Today
marriage looks like
twin sunset-sailed wind
surfers closely parallel
on a placid sea
mosttimes upright
sometimes over
raretimes one

New Lane: The Flaggy Meadow
for Lucille Pew

In midwinter, it bears the weight
of countless skaters, all ages;
they whirl and fall, shout and pass,
unaware of the secret blue glory
inches beneath their blades.

Ice melts, seasons change, and the place
becomes only damp green among greens.
The ordinary eye skims over it, heedless
as those flashing skates, and moves on.

But come early June, those of us who know,
take detours, watch eagerly, wait patiently
for just this few days' revelation.
It is like being present at the Transfiguration of Christ:
such a sight once seen
makes one faith full for life

Evening at the White Elephant

They are at it again—
my Zeus and our Athena—
lost in a wilderness of candles
and wine glasses,
oblivious to the rest of us.

Ram against lion, conflict arises
over almost anything: feminism,
philosophy, opposing views of history.

Worse than a Roman circus, these
strident storms of words.

The others watch, interject and applaud,
although I soon cease to listen:
water in a jostled goblet leaps up,
but does not spill,
and the tall swanneck shadow of a ficus
on the high white wall behind them
never moves.

Over Dinner

They are talking about bodies:
injuries, accidents, pain,
emergency rooms and ski patrols,
the necessary detachment
to be learned in anatomy class.

It is still light, and
beyond our full-length windows
two bodies arrest my absent glance:
a leaping, sprawling child on a trampoline
'way up through tall brush on Hinckley Lane,
and the red streak of a male cardinal
passing close, north-south, across our hilltop yard.
I am seeing effort and surrender;
I am seeing the speed of one-pointed attention;
and where the horizontal meets the vertical
on this most personal radar screen,
I am seeing a third body, also;
one pure enough and strong enough to bear
the sufferings of the whole world.

Is this how the living moment expands—
everything becoming of the deepest significance?
Will He continue to be the central focus, always;
is that another part of His promise I can trust,
from now on?

Summer Song

The ultimate ocean is the name
of the Lord
Come   Let us sport like seals
bask like sharks and sunfish
sound and breach like whales

Deeper and deeper the father carries
his child into roiling boisterous waves
Tighter and tighter she clings
                              smiles

II. FALL

Labor Day

Always, there is more joy;
even dreams of Paradise have not prepared these eyes
 for the sight of a beach plum tree at harvesttime.

I circle this singular festival of multi-
colored lights   (a palette from picture books,
children's rhymes and fairytales come alive)
plucking the ripest little globes only,
thinking besides thank you, oh thank you;
bring on the clowns, the swordswallower,
the tiger leaping through a ring of fire;
how better to extend this stationary celebration
unless on my knees, in silence.

A glimpse of marsh grass, tidal pond and low dunes;
a certain sweep of moor;
how many thousands but this that breathless one
which sees the everpresent perfection.

Losing speech, perhaps soon reason;
until I am living wild among the burning bushes
saying   Behold, behold
to all who pass by.

Madaket Clambake

We are speaking of sunsets
my new friend and I
out on the westernmost beach this incomparable evening
watching variable light smite sea oats
sand dunes   west-facing windows above tall grass
Each moment another blow
driving the nail home   Forget the heart
says Suzi   this place attacks one's very soul

We discuss Nantucket like lovers a beloved
like drunkards their favorite wine
Were we all once Indians   whalers
tourists   traders   Quakers
who never saw enough of this misty sandspit
thirty miles at sea
and thus had to come back

The sun leaves behind mesmerizing red striations
until stars pop out loud as gunshots
and a half moon sloshes silver on dark water
to walk on   oh, to walk on   straight
into the beyond

Some yearn to stay here year round   I do now
and long only for God

Steamed island corn   a sleepy child   fire-animated faces
Everything's filled with summer'send sweetness
I could see it still if I became suddenly blind

The Assault

The one I live with   full of sorrows
readies the contents of his quiver
and lets fly
arrow after poison-tipped arrow
straight at my heart
                    But I am filled
with sparkling seas and curving sands
with yellow flowers against a fence
and huge translucent clouds

                            a cry
of love so loud it drowns out
all possible else

The small child shakes his fists
flings dirt at the sky
                    which only smiles
then pours down even more star fall
and moon shine

The Fall

I lost my self in the water this summer
Day after glorious day
I entered into the dance of love I saw
all around me
                The sea the wind the
sky the cross-like drops of light
even the big grey-shingled houses
up on the bluff swayed
to that timeless music and I knew
the joy of feeling totally at home

The soon off to school again girl child
nestles close against my heart Would climb
back inside the womb if she could
                I am the same
until the first strong chills announce
the body has had enough of today's
rough buoyancy

And now stands heavy and bereft
on cold dry land

After Nantucket There Is Only God

August is the hardest
We are tied to clients houseguests or garden
able to flee only occasionally
to a favorite outlying beach

All summer long our little town's infected
with bigcity habits and expectations
so many vacationers struggling to have a good time
burdened by far more than their luggage   vehicles
windsurfers   skateboards and bikes

But Labor Day comes and most of them go
No more discouraging lines at the Post Office
the markets
or jams at the cenotaph on Upper Main Street
No more frantic frustrating obstacle races
to make Federal Express
Rare mopeds or runners   pleasant pedestrians
There's finally time to smell the late roses
watch the last blackberries ripen
collect wild pears   rosehips   plums

In fall a sacred net is cast over the entire
                                                island
It's then the true holy days begin
Daily the silence deepens   and the sea
the moors   the marshes and the light
The clear quiet inside spreads
Stars brighten   and our faces as we wrap
ourselves in ever-increasing stillness
to rise beyond the always of this place

Cisco Beach: Hurricane

Gloria, that marvelous raging sculptress,
has unveiled five monks at prayer
beneath the grass at Cisco Beach.

At the base of a ragged, striated bank
they stand
        beings of root, earth, sand.
Salt rime outlines the folds of their robes.

No Burghers of Calais these, but close.

Come let us nestle between their knees
and share their silence, their view
of low blue clouds and liquid light
then close our own eyes
and watch the inner sky open,   open.

Not Yet

Lately
Smith's Point has become a state of mind

Off we go in a high bright wind
and the red Dreadnought   no top
thundering across this sandy Siberia
on balloon tires
soft enough not to squash a child's foot
Dark blue frothing down the outside
light blue calm down the inside

From the crest of the planted dune
at the near end
(Gloria swept away nary one blade)
it seems all of a piece   finally united
the Point and Esther's Isle   but no
Up close in damp gravel a deep swift
narrow channel still separates
divides
and I am flung back suddenly
into the Sistine Chapel
weeping   weeping at the immense distance
between two fingers

Attachment

Since birth I've endured a suffocation of swans
on my breast
Despite many attempts to get rid of them
they settled in   rested nested brooded and preened
Nothing I ever did budged them

Today swiftly silently   quite without effort
or warning they all left
Only a single soft white feather to tell
of past presence

To have breath come unencumbered even once

Portrait Of A Young Man

Out in the urban world   he
is like a beached seal
still able to breath   move   do
but in great need
                        Frightened
big eyes dark with innocence
Wary
big eyes blank from confusion

What strand team's member
will come to raise him up
toss him back   blissful
into the inner sea
                        and when
Oh   let it be soon

Polpis Harbor

It is a placid perfect sunsink
scalloping boats grow there
                              and a few
small sails
Also stormcombed grasses
the shades of many marmalades

At the edge of still water   startled
from his contemplation   a heron silhouette
hesitates   glides off   lands further away
and immediately returns to immobility
He faces the trees   not the shallows
may be through thinking about food

I should have such dedication

Five wide indistinct fingers of light reach
across pale blue from west to east
                              casting me back
to Dehra Dun   watching another sun set just
behind the head of the one who made the sun
Its fan of goldenwhite   the orb itself big
and bright beyond my best dreams   I left
those loving gracefilled eyes over and over
mesmerized

That brief painted glory was his gift I know
but what did I miss   oh, what did I miss

October On Nantucket

Oh Columbus!
This island teems with devotees
come to worship the burning moors
the molten cobalt sea
                      They build
elaborate historically accurate sand
castles   Raise sailors knots and whales
Adorn a dozing mermaid with a necklace
of broken quahog shells   garland beachpeas
in her wheatstraw hair
                         Wear boutonnieres
of heather   then stride from kame to kettle-
hole dreaming of Ireland
                      When a wind rises
                      toward dusk
they skate   arms wide as flight   or cycle
unseeing in great lazy arcs
down empty side streets
They are up and about at odd hours
walking   jogging   listening   gazing
                         Do they
receive the glance of grace which passed
over this little land not long ago
                         or hear
the light tread of one whose holy feet
made every brick and window tremble

Oh Columbus!
This island teems with devotees

Water Color

for Beverly Hall

Yesterday the late peach and mauve light was clear
enough to see Hyannis like widely spaced satellites
strung along a sharp horizon thirty miles away

Today in steady rain it is these furry cliffs nearby
which catch and hold our glance   a sweep of skulking
summer mink above seaweedstrewn sand
an amazement of browns   One's gaze caresses it
like some beloved household pet
                                              moves on
to varying grey striations of clay
                                              then down
to sparse bursts of eelgrass at their base
tall thin curving fires of orange   cream   jade green

This subtle autumn palette's a new wine
We are quite drunk before returning home

Last spring a pale English finger of sun
showing me yellow primroses on mosspocked banks
And a flood of bluebells in a holy wood
almost brought me senseless to the ground

Tears cleanse error from the heart and loving
attention intensifies

Now I study a spangled night sky and hear you say
you want to see stars   I shall reveal stars
just close your eyes
for many   brighter   and much more

Oh my joy   What extremity of beauty will it take
to make me leave all outer sights behind   as though
struck suddenly Damascus blind

Thanksgiving 1984

Quickly   he is far ahead of us
striding along   sometimes jogging
intent only on his destination
oblivious to everything   red berries
rabbits   sunset   mysterious hedges
a shock of springgreen lawn
Neither looks around
nor checks behind
as fixed on the looming striped lighthouse
as I became fifteen years ago
on another hidden light

But the womanchild's stylish boots
were made for envy or admiration
not this swift three-mile hike
I stay close until her smiling   bye Mom
frees me
to run and run   walk fast panting then run
again
never giving cry   wait   please
oh, wait for me
how many times soundless down the seasons
his heart the same

til in the light's shadow we're in step
                              at last

At Tom Never's Head

Full gale blowing
cold whistling winds   low dark clouds   heaving flood
waters and spectacular spindrift
whole great gauzy strips of it
floating past at each foaming crest
too fragile to last   like rare ancient manuscripts
which collapse when exposed to open air
But I am reading the sea more deeply today
For sitting here on a driftwood pole
sorely buffeted and ignoring it   is like
looking into the eyes of the incarnation
like being drawn right inside
to face directly that majestic surging restlessness
which fills and covers the entire universe

No longer a hunched and shuddering bundle
obstructing the passage of invisible fierceness
up this empty beach
A bird   rather   riding high thermals
a lark at first sunsight

Approaching The Cave
for Arlene O'Reilly

I am hemmed in by metaphors
The this-is-thatness of all which surrounds me
demands my constant attention   reminds
me again and again of the true purpose of life

I strip to dress for work and sweat
pants and socks rounded with winter static
dance upon the bathroom door
leaving me without a body in the office

As I walk the empty offseason beach a single
watchful surfer riding then falling
eagerly spread-eagled back into the sea becomes
an ecstatic soul dropping into the lap of God

I read of Newgrange   of elaborate passage graves
of an axis and roof box aligned to catch and briefly hold
the sun at winter solstice

                                  Oh Ireland
I am a passage grave   unadorned
My heart is high priest
a slain mind the sacrifice
The roof box above my eyes not yet opened
as I wait for His light not once a year only but
day after night after day

III. WINTER

Nantucket Monochrome

Oh my iceblue   grassgold   mostly
black and white island
winter has stolen the sound of the sea
imprisoned the waves
cast whippedcream lava upon the north strand

I am inebriated with greyness
at one with all cold places
but here the air is so much dancing light
nothing to catch or clutter the eye
vistas of infinity

Interior Landscape

From the cliff tip   white is all I see
far past the jetty   the last buoy
the sweep of Coatue
then a thin line of blue
five points look frozen and the entire
inner harbor's cold and still

At this distance access seems
impossible   but down on the beach
slow motion in the icebound channel

and morning sun strong behind light
clouds

Like A Beacon On High

Like a beacon on high his gaze sweeps
across this crowd seated before him
We watch and wait   We barely breathe
And when that beam of perfect peace
strikes each wide open mind
we know ourselves to be
in the presence of Eternity

Steadily we pitch and toss toward him

'Sconset Beach

Don't worry   I know how to swim
I told my companion as I dove right in
But the afterstorm undertow was very strong
and I fell asleep   got swept far down
into a series of strange small sandscalloped
coves with steep brown walls and a rising sea
I kept diving back in   convinced the familiar length
of beach lay just around the next arc
The sea still rising   rising
Tiring finally   and alarmed   I recognize No
that is not the way
I turn and climb then   scramble up on hands and knees
hope the crumbling bare dark ridge holds
Am I on firm land   a fastdisappearing island
the spine of a dragon
Will he have to send a plane
                              a pteradactyl

Surfside: State Forest

We have come to collect Christmas greens
but find instead
Love rushing toward us
from damp cool air   dark silent trees
spiky thicklycushioned ground
like an intimate family gathered to greet
some longawaited kin
Gleeful yet reverent I dance across patches
of swirling redgold grass to hug
one stationary member   bow low before another
then hold my breath
for anything could happen in here next
I think if I dug deep enough
I would discover empty space
this forest just a pocket of mystery
made manifest for my pleasure today

I need no shears   pine cones abound
and many sprays and branches gifted to us
by a clipping wind   Our errand is quickly done

Let us hide little bells all over
then go away   suggests my Russian artist friend
but a string of small white mushrooms rings
at my feet
            and the clamor of clumps of blackened
Indian pipes   each a tiny cathedral bombed by frost
is deafening
                I have to bear it   bear all and sing
whatever is inside is found also outside

Will I penetrate my mother's mirror or someday
break it
Surely this place is one step further
toward the ultimate embrace

The Flotation Device

for Tamarra Kaida

He has enticed his latest conquest   reluctant
fearful   restless and depressed   dizzy with living
from a far desert place and set her down
on our tiny island
                    "for a rest"

Privy for once to another's seduction I watch
inevitable hows and whys become awe and ahhh
as he woos her daily with subtle sunsets   storm
clouds   spindrift and mists never seen
in her chosen land of continuous blue and saguaro

He courts her in forms he knows she holds
particularly dear
hawk   pheasant   swan   owl   goose sometimes petting
close   all things that fly as she is dying to
Even sends aloft banners of mallards although
it's not a script she can decipher
Her husband's the scientist

She stumbles through bleached eelgrass
down along empty beaches so full of light
 she cannot distinguish earth from air
taking pictures   making notes
wide open
Each day's the best

Ecstasy is exhausting   she says   then cries
more moon to a black night sky

He makes himself small enough to inhabit
moonsnails and scallopshells
which she brings home by the bowlful
to fondle and dream over like so many loveletters

Hourly he caresses her   calms her without touch or word

Her favorite place is the narrowing neck
between natural dunes and planted ones
at the west end
On the outside vivid striped skies
above foaming capering waves and shoals
On the inside   across great flats
stillness and tranquility
She smiles   sighs   sees herself most clearly here
Both sides

One day she turns away from the drama of still-rising
Whale Island and nearer gale-reduced
dunes   edges
toward the placid expanse embraced by Eel Point
and stands pillared
as a wind becomes a swift small boat
our attention skiers taut behind
in a sudden funneled flow of all creation
into a single bright spot on the far horizon
Perhaps   I think   she's finally seen him
undisguised
arms opened wide

Look   she says   breathless   It wants us
Barefoot already I advance
while she stoops quickly to remove her shoes

New Year's Eve

Our intimate highminded dialogue breaks
off   I begin to stare   for suddenly
silently the room is filling with peace
like a lock chamber in a canal
like a flood plain below an open dam

The air thrums and there is sweetest music
from beyond the three worlds
As we breathe it all increases
silence   thrumming   music   peace

A fish made of wind   I swim
up into it   and it is in me   surrounds me
motionless on a chair

Nearby the youngmanson   round brown
eyes five again
asks
If I pray   will anyone hear

On Lincoln's Birthday

Frozen foam scallops the north beach
A thick rumpled sheet stretches from the end
of the jetty all the way past Eel Point
to Tuckernuck
              White and still
Except for the low thundering train
under the distant open blue   ceaseless
and muffled as in a snowy mountain pass
inexorable as an avalanche once begun

It is like the secret thing in my heart
steadily moving   although yet unseen

The pink sky lifts   spreads   then sighs
Just you wait

In Our Back Yard

Late February sun
slowly melts old snow
Green shoots thrust up
through wind-dispersed mulch
A cock pheasant struts and crows

At Hummock Pond

Like blown trash around the dump last patches
of old snow untidy the goldredsablebrown landscape
The pond is high and made of melted wax
Reeds along its far edge an ogham script in the mist
Two diamond ducks cut from south to north toward
an osprey nest on a pole
and the sweet salt watermelonsmelling afterstorm air
is a feast to make one quickly replete

On the near side of those fading cinnamon distances
a surging thundering sea reaches   reaches
across the low narrow band of sand between
A few minutes   it seems   from union

Even as I lie down   deeply still   awaiting
the waves of your grace

Long Pond

Signs and portents in the sky tonight
Phoenix wings and rising herons
The spent skin of the worm
Ouroboros fast disappearing as the Concorde booms
softly toward the other side of the world

Then dense neon pink fire long and high
in the west
               a threat or a promise of
               heaven or hell

What is the fate of this scruffy little sand
pile thirty miles at sea
awash with dirty money and greed
sustained by patient lonely devotion
Which one is increasing

Meanwhile the white swans feed and preen on Long
Pond
Red berries brighten bare brambles   branches
Bleached grasses edge clear blue water
and there is no wind

Beyond The Shells

for Lisa Frey

Instead of meditating,
Allowing one-pointed attention on the holy Sound
To pull us, lift us, drag us up   up
Right out of this world,
We bungee jump and ski,
We wind surf and hang glide,
Or kite board —
Nineteen feet high in the air
Off the seething crest
Of a southeasterly breeze -
Driven wave —

                                        Oh

Who would choose to leave
Such wonderfully turbulent water,
Ever.

We long so much to fly.

Aside from magic—occult powers
Known as riddhis and siddhis in the East—
Those so-called slaves of concentration,
The body does rise quite naturally
Sometimes,
  Inches   even feet
Under ideal conditions:
All fears and appetites quelled,
Mind perfectly still,
Heart surrendered completely
To the divine,
But it is only the soul that truly flies,
My wet-suited, sea (and seal)-skimming friend,
It's our immortal soul that
  Most   truly
                          flies.

VI. SPRING

What Happened To Great Point Light?

We saw it all   said the gulls   the terns   in their sodden
                nests
We watched it fall

The waves were high
They ate the sand
The white thing leaned
It could not stand

We saw it all said they said they
We watched it fall

We heard it all said the new green shoots in the tossing
                grass
We heard it fall

The wind was strong
It pushed and pushed
The white thing crumbled
in a thundering rush

We heard it all said they said they
We heard it fall

We felt it all said the shells and stones and fishy bones
            up the beach for miles
We felt it fall

The rain was hard
It soaked deep in
The white thing's heaped
as if it had never been
tall and bright throughout the night
for long long years

We felt it fall said they said they
We felt it all

The Jetties

Definitely
the egg came first
like one for Russian Easter
only painted inside
Seamless landscapes of sea and sky
filled with sloth and iniquity
It is too small
but I cannot crack it open alone

Bright Green

In soft island rain   the impatiens
the brick sidewalks   even small weeds
at the base of great trees
sing
        Hosannah
        Hosannah

More In Madaket

Dense April fog
Down behind the houses we walk
a narrow strip of beach
between silvery grass
and oblivion
No feeding or basking seals
no Esther's Isle   no Eel Point
across the multishaded shallows
only intense white light
swirling around a pulsating yellow eye
and the roar of a not distant cataract
at the edge of the known world

The man examines his watch   turns back
His coat is the color of sand   His pants
the redbrown of the just-budding moors

I follow

March Storm

It doesn't take much to make the redness
come
       One good rain
and all the old tall grasses are sherry
the hawthorns claret moors burgundy
We become greedy omnibibulous
Pale green stubble's still only sparse
on the chin of south dunes
Deeper more profligate in fields
Crocus and snowdrop already present on
Centre Street

The whole island swells with life
like a dry stick moving straight
into flames

The mild air keens and sighs
the sky weeps for the light
            and when it shows
suddenly
      below the forever grey
we are facing at least creation day one or
a stray inner sun

Easter: Wind With Junipers

Learning to be a tree
is easy
        Just plant your
self deeply in Him
then frolic
in His greeting

❦

Daffodils

for Granger Frost

The old house itself is a treasuretrove
but we seek living gold this chilly April day

Down to his overstocked fishpond   spots where he watches
birds   up around a loop of lawn among dense hawthorns
we follow our tall stooped host

In the most secluded thickets luxurious clusters nod
huge heads and wave as we pass

Beside Lost Creek's mats of red grass mosses throb
like organs and an entire congregation of yellow and white
sing alleluiahs to the steadily strengthening sun

He has cleared vast amounts of brush but lets it rot
to enrich the soil   planted and protected dogwood
rhododendron   feeds countless birds
There's more to do in there always

The place is a map of the man

More Lessons

Housebound   all day
working and praying   then out
into a conflagration of clouds and dazzling light
                 to convince me again
have patience   faith
Heaven's just one perfect prayer away

Out later into darkness and high wind
to face a black plastic demon
and abject slave
escaped from Gerry's truck
bowing and scraping
expanding and collapsing
my own Wicked Witch of the West

Oh man   never forget   death is on your head

The Daffodil Festival

Oh people   Have you come to see God
His benedictions abound here

His glance wrought the nodding white
and gold magic along Milestone Road   along
the way to Polpis   Warren's Landing and
Smith's Point

Behind every burst of forsythia lies
His open hand

In predawn silence His voice can be heard
bells outside of church
flutes without concert
thunder and no suggestion of storm

In lapping low tide He smiles

Sunlight and stars even in the rain

April On Nantucket

Babbling daffodils   festooned with forsythia
the old grey lady waltzes toward May

As icy winds diminish   chilly fogs withdraw
As her acres and acres of bare bayberry   of
hawthorn thickets just come into bud
Yellow   yellow   yellow she trills
and throws her arms wide   (Robins and rabbits
pheasant and deer tumble from her mantle)

Oh Faraway Isle   no matter who the comers or
livers
you will always embrace   these vivid simple
manifestations of grace

Much More Than Spring

The boss has spring fever   leaves
a machine in charge of his law office
takes his happy amanuensis to an empty beach
to watch seals bob and dive in liquid light
peninsula stretch toward hurricane island
The wind   the scalloping water shifting two fingers
closer   closer
                 gulls and sandpipers the only other
witnesses to this moving image from the Sistine Chapel

Across Hither Creek the missing sick forest
at Warren's Landing's a scar upon my own breast
Pussywillows near the dump   the deepening redness
in the moors seem to sprout this year
from my own heart   and every eyeful's a reminder
much more than spring approaches

Oh   much more than spring approaches

Easy Street Basin

Look at them   the infatuated ones
struck dumb and still as dock pilings
by a small vista of sailboats   dories
greyshingled cottages on stilts
cement dolphins and a glimpse of low Coatue
across calm water

But it's May and who can blame them
The old lady's decked out in dizzying greens
and blues and flowers
her rabbits and pheasant tame as city pigeons

Come back in March or January   I long to tell them
Live here when she sheds her lavish finery
and her bare bones show
when cold wet winds lash her bleak and scruffy
barrenness
and there's nothing to do but go inside
Be brave   I long to tell them
Find out if your summer love is true

The Bottle Plant

This invited, welcomed guest
(ordered from Thompson & Morgan, The Seedsmen)
arrived in a small, flat, padded paper packet,
like a tape from an earlier age.

Its jadepale leaves — no two the same shape —
were folded: delicate as dragonfly wings
or origami.

But the huge root was too much a mandrake's,
and I wondered how to plant
without it suffocating.

An appropriate vessel was soon found:
round and deep with a bamboo motif
which mirrored its own brown and green.

Once potted,
the exposed part of the root become trunk
resembled a headless brontosaurus at rest.

I watched its placid, monstrous stance
for over a week;
the foliage remained closed.

Today it was given its first drink;
water containing minute amounts
of a common household potion known as
"Miracle-Gro."

By evening,
the dinosaur had disappeared inside the bowl,
in its place I find a dainty Japanese
with flowing silks, holding two fans:
there is a blustery, fitful wind; her hair's
unbound, and she is dancing, dancing.

At Cisco Beach: "The Ark" Is Claimed By The Sea

The love of God is relentless:
Man's ignorance, arrogance, self-pity
cannot stand against it indefinitely.
The mind is like a great house built on sand;
daily wind and water scoop away
the supporting bank,
until one certain storm comes
which wrenches the building apart,
causes the thing to topple into the sea
then sweeps the beach clean.
No individuality remains.

A Gardener's Catalogue

Let me tell you about Kaufmanniana tulips, Alfred Cortot:
they are large, low and red.
When fully opened, they are hot, bright, six-pointed stars;
satin petals arched almost flat
to catch the deepest penetration of the light.
They care nothing about winds or honey bees,
or starved, nibbling deer;
even with bits missing, their whole attention
is on maximum exposure to the sun.
More glorious than those depicted in Persian miniatures,
they fit at least one saint's description
of a God-intoxicated soul:
living flames of love.

But tightly-closed toward night or under cloudy skies,
they become an attack of arrows
as I devotedly approach.
Back, back: go back inside, they admonish me;
we are only a pale reflection,
mere reminders of Paradise.
You should be looking at the real thing.

Still Life With Daffodils

In the center of our spacious kitchen, this web:
a chair, a throw, a wall-hanging on a broad column,
a table and a flower-filled vase.
Five disparate items, you say, and shrug: so what?
You need more information and much prayer
to see what I see:
                     strong threads of love binding,
binding this comfortable walnut sculpture,
a Stephen Swift rocker,
to my sister's crocheted wool scallops,
to a small round piece of my mother-in-law's,
some delicate mahogany hand, rising up
from a white pool of Irish rug,
cupped to hold only something very precious:
that hobnailed glass of daffodils;
                         (yell, oh!
in days and days of April fog, these have become
our sun)
to my mother's fine bright needlepoint,
a tall Jacobean Tree of Life, behind,
and across the room at last, to me.

It is a kind of still life, if you will,
except there's no such thing.
They've been made with love, by love; they are forms
of love and it is love also which sits watching
its total explosion.

Would you believe me if I said
it was better than a manifestation of angels?
Would you believe me if I said
it was almost like looking at our Master's face?
Am I, happiest of captives, going to kneel
like this, soon, before everything?

Tracy Leddy was born in Boston, Massachusetts in 1940, graduated from Wheaton College, Norton, Massachusetts and received her Montessori Diploma from Sion Hill Convent, Dublin, Ireland. She also holds a Master's degree in education from the Peaceable Schools Program at Lesley University.

A long-time resident of Nantucket Island, Massachusetts, Tracy was initiated into Surat Shabd Yoga, a meditation practice of the Sound Current, by Sant Kirpal Singh in 1969. She spent many years visiting Sant Ajaib Singh, Kirpal's Successor, and more recently began making frequent trips to India to benefit from the presence and teachings of the living master, Sant Sadhu Ram.

Tracy is the author of two other published works: *Allison's Shadow*, and a companion volume, *The Song of Everything*. Both have been translated into German; *Allison's Shadow* has been translated into Italian. The first edition of *October on Nantucket* was published in 1987 and quickly went out of print. This second edition of *October on Nantucket* is available in print, ebook, and audio book form. Please visit our website, quailhillpublishing.com, for further details.

www.quailhillpublishing.com

Made in the USA
Charleston, SC
28 November 2012